Disney · PIXAR

BRAVE

THE ESSENTIAL GUIDE

Disney · PIXAR

BRAVE

THE ESSENTIAL GUIDE

Written by Barbara Bazaldua

Contents

Introduction

In the Highlands of Scotland, where mystical circles of stone guard ancient secrets, tales are told of daring deeds, strange spells, and legendary creatures. There, in a castle high above the craggy cliffs and misty glens, lives Merida, the bold Princess of DunBroch. This is her story… from a time when magic is as real as a castle's stone walls, and a wish can become the beginning of a legend told by flickering firelight, while will o' the wisps beckon to be followed.

Perfect Protection

Long ago, the castle's stone walls and towers were built for protection. The land is at peace now, but the towers still make the family feel safe, like strong, stone guards.

Turrets

Merida loves this landscape. She comes here to practice her archery, or just climb a tree and sit and think.

Stone bridge

Games Field

The Highland Games Field is where all the kingdom's clans traditionally gather each year for contests of might and skill. It gets very competitive.

Castle DunBroch

Welcome to Castle DunBroch. Merida lives here with her parents, the King and Queen, and her three bothersome brothers. The castle has been around for hundreds of years and she thinks it's the fairest place in all the world.

Merida's brothers love to stand on top of the gatehouse and pour buckets of cold water on visitors.

Fergus calls this tower his "bear den," because he can take long naps here undisturbed—except when his sons are nearby.

When her mother's not busy bossing everyone, she comes here to gather plants for dyes and medicines.

Steep cliffs

Inside the Walls

Clan Dunbroch has everything it needs inside the castle walls, including a stable. Merida's horse Angus always hurries back there after a day exploring.

Maudie, the maid, serves the family in the dining hall. Meals aren't exactly peaceful, but they're always interesting.

Gordon and Martin guard the castle's main entrance. No bears allowed!

Fergus has stuffed the halls with stuffed bears. It's his idea of decorating.

The Grand Tour

Merida's family has lived in Castle DunBroch for generations. It's full of secret passages and rooms no one knows about (except her brothers), but there's lots more to explore in this stony structure. Come take a look...

Elinor made this tapestry to show the DunBrochs woven together, like a family should be.

Elinor and Merida spend hours together in the tapestry room, talking, laughing—and sometimes arguing.

Merida's bedroom is big enough for her to practice swordplay techniques. She likes swords a lot better than dresses!

The Great Hall is used for big events like the gathering of the clans.

Who wants to sit in a castle acting prim and proper? Not Merida! She prefers to roam the Highlands.

Merida

High-spirited Merida loves her freedom and fiercely defies her mother's attempts to turn her into the "perfect princess." Bold and independent, Merida is determined to find her own path in life, but she must first learn the meaning of true courage.

LIKES:
- Riding her horse, Angus
- Archery practice
- Sword fighting lessons with her father

DISLIKES:
- Dressing up
- Combing her hair
- Learning to act like a princess
- Her mother's lectures

Hot Headed
Merida says what she's thinking—often loudly! The outspoken lass has a temper and spirit as fiery as her vivid red hair.

Princess Act
Merida may have to dress up for the clan gathering, but she doesn't have to like it! When her Mum isn't looking, Merida lets her hair do its own thing.

"I want my freedom!" Merida

Merida carries her bow and quiver of arrows around with her—just in case!

Hot Shot

King Fergus gave Merida her first bow when she was a tiny lass and it is her most beloved possession. An expert archer, Merida can hit a bullseye even from her galloping horse. Her suitors don't stand a chance!

Feud-all Family

Merida gets along great with her father, however she clashes with her controlling mother and wishes she would change.

No frills, please! Merida likes simple dresses she can romp, ride, and roam in.

Queen Elinor

Elinor's crown sparkles with jade.

Decorous and diplomatic, Queen Elinor rules the castle, the kingdom, and her family with a firm hand in a velvet glove. With calm graciousness, she manages everything and everyone—except her beloved but unruly daughter.

Family Portrait

One of Merida's fondest memories is watching Elinor stitch the family tapestry that symbolizes the threads of love and tradition that bind them.

Elinor likes traditions and correct behavior, which explains why she dislikes Merida's untamed ways so much.

Did You Know?

The name Elinor means "shining light."

Brains Behind the Brawn

While Fergus blusters, Elinor plans. The far-sighted Queen's political skills are just as important as Fergus's strength in keeping the kingdom peaceful and prosperous.

"We can't just run away from who we are." Elinor

The Look

Elinor would never dream of raising her voice. But when she gives "the look," everyone, including Fergus, straightens up.

Elinor and Fergus may seem like an odd couple, but she keeps him calm, and he makes her laugh.

If You'd Just Listen…

Elinor wants Merida to marry and invites the neighboring Lords' sons to the castle to compete for Merida's hand. But Merida wants her freedom. They both have a point. If they could just listen to each other…

Family Fun

Elinor and Fergus have created a family full of loving care. No matter what happens, they all have a special bond.

Elinor's elegant green gown reflects her cool poise and regal calm.

15

King Fergus

Brawny, blustering King Fergus is a courageous warrior, benevolent leader, and caring husband and father. Down-to-earth Fergus lives life with gusto. He has a hearty sense of humor, but when it comes to protecting his family, he's bold as a bear.

Beware the Bear

Fergus loves bellowing his song about his legendary battle with Mor'du, the demon bear who took his leg. He vows that someday, he'll turn the beast into a rug!

Like Father, Like Daughter

Merida gets more than just her red hair from her adoring dad. She's also inherited Fergus's bold, outgoing spirit and sense of fun.

Warrior King

With his strength and courage, King Fergus united the clans and together they vanquished their enemies. Under his benevolent rule, the kingdom has enjoyed years of peace… until now.

Did You Know?

The name Fergus means "strong man."

Called a "Gillie brogue," Fergus' traditional leather shoe keeps his foot dry when he's hunting.

"Then out of nowhere, the biggest bear you've ever seen!" Fergus

LIKES:
- Battles, brawls, and hunting
- Singing about his battle with Mor'du
- Big dinners

DISLIKES:
- Talk of magic spells and curses
- The demon bear, Mor'du
- Worrying about table manners

Fergus's wooden leg is carved from yew wood. It's as strong as the rest of him.

Big Kid
A big, boisterous kid at heart, Fergus never lets his peg leg stop him from enjoying a hunt or a good-natured brawl. It's all in the spirit of fun!

The Legend

Elinor believes that Merida must choose a suitor in order to keep peace in the kingdom. Trying to make her unwilling daughter accept her responsibilities as the Princess of DunBroch, Elinor tells her favorite cautionary tale. But Merida's heard it all before.

Chaos and Ruin

Once there was an ancient kingdom ruled by a wise, fair king. When he grew old, he divided the kingdom among his four sons. The oldest prince wanted to rule the land for himself so the kingdom fell to war, chaos, and ruin.

Chess Bored

Elinor places chess pieces on the four corners of a table with a chessboard resting on top. She pulls the prince's piece out and the board and pieces crash down. Elinor wants to shock Merida, but it doesn't work.

"That's a nice story."
Merida

Merida is so bored by Elinor's tale that you can almost hear her roll her eyes. This dusty old story isn't going to change her mind.

"Legends are lessons. They ring with truths." Elinor

Stalemate Situation

Merida argues furiously, but Elinor stands firm: "I would advise you to make your peace with this." The discussion ends typically—with a slammed door.

Troubled Elinor tells Fergus that she wishes Merida would listen to her. Ironically, Merida feels the same way about her mother and confides in her best friend Angus.

Clan Colors

Each clan traditionally has a symbol and a unique plaid design that is woven into fabric. Plaids are very helpful during brawls, so clansmen don't accidentally punch their own family members.

A scabbard can be tied to a leather strap if needed.

Kilts don't have pockets so a sporran acts as a wallet.

Dingwall

- The Dingwall clan hails from an extremely rocky Highland area, which explains Dingwall's hardheadedness.
- Dingwall tartan colors represent the thistle and heather from the Highland countryside.
- Some Dingwalls are small of stature and more apt to try to prove themselves.

The Dingwall symbol is the stone, an ancient relic held by the clan.

MacGuffin

- The MacGuffin clan comes from a rainy coastal area, so their tartans smell like wet sheep.
- MacGuffin tartan colors are inspired by the hillsides of heather found in the Highland country.
- Clan MacGuffin traditionally wears a studded leather undershirt for extra armor.

The MacGuffin symbol resembles a cauldron, an ancient magical relic said to have fed thousands of warriors in battle.

A chain mail shirt adds an extra layer of protection.

The leather strap secures the scabbard of his broad sword.

Sporrans are usually made from leather or bear fur.

DunBroch

- The DunBroch clan comes from a region of lochs, which inspires the blue color.
- DunBroch tartan colors are inspired by the Kilt Rock, a rock formation on the Isle of Skye.

The DunBroch family symbol represents bravery and the protection of the kingdom.

Macintosh

- The Macintosh clan is from an area near the Isle of Skye.
- The clan grows apples when not fighting, hence the red, yellow, and green in its plaid.
- Clan Macintosh wears traditional blue war paint to inspire fear.

The Macintosh symbol resembles an ancient lyre with powers summoned by a musical note.

Three's Trouble

Merida's younger brothers, Princes Hamish, Hubert, and Harris, are identical triplets who take mischief-making to new heights. The unstoppable, fearless little tricksters seem to spend their days planning new ways to wreak hilarious havoc in the castle.

Perpetually hungry, the triplets are always nabbing nibbles from the kitchen. Playing pranks takes fuel!

Big Sister

The triplets may tease Merida, but they also look up to her, and when she needs help, the boys are delighted to assist.

Wee little clansmen-in-training, the triplets wear kilts in the family tartan.

LIKES:
- Playing tricks on Maudie the maid
- Muffins, muffins, and more muffins

DISLIKES:
- Squishy food like porridge and haggis

"They get away with murder." Merida

Castle Explorers

The rowdy little ruffians know every nook and cranny of the castle. Their knowledge is useful when Merida needs help escaping the castle.

The triplets have heads of red curls, just like their sister.

Little Rascals

The triplets show a real flair for inventing new tricks to play, like the scary bear shadow they create using a chicken from the kitchen!

Did You Know?

Identical triplets are very rare. Only about three per cent of triplets are identical.

DO
aim to win.
If you feel like a winner,
you will be a winner—
hopefully!

DO NOT
let go of your bow when you
let go of the arrow! You don't
want your shot to flop.

Merida's Top Tips for Ace Archery & Swordplay

Merida loves archery and swordplay, and she's
one very skillful princess. Her father has taught
her everything he knows, but Merida has also
learned some essential tips and tricks on her own.

DO
use both hands to hold and swing a heavy broadsword. Dropping a sword on your foot is not a good move.

DO NOT
swing a sword inside the castle, even if you're angry. Tapestries and sharp edges don't mix.

DO
grip your horse with your knees when firing a bow and arrow. Staying on your horse is much more fun than falling off.

DO
learn your dueling opponents' weak spots—like your dad's wooden leg—and go for them. Chop! Chop!

DO
practice swordplay with a true master, like your dad. It's the best way to sharpen your skills.

DO NOT
get distracted, even if your dress is too tight and your Mum is yelling at you. Concentrate!

Angus

Strong, intelligent, and loyal, Angus is always ready to canter around the Highlands with Merida. They are so close, he can anticipate her every move as she practices shooting targets with her bow and arrow from his back. After all that exercise, he is glad to return to his stable and a bucket of oats at night.

Nervous Nag

Angus loves adventures with Merida, but the bold horse balks near the Ring of Stones. It makes the hairs on his tail prickle.

Caring Companion

Merida doesn't let anyone else care for Angus. She feeds, waters, and brushes him herself. It's what best friends do.

Angus is so strong and large that he can easily carry Merida and her three brothers all at once.

Did You Know?
Angus is a medieval breed of horse called a Clydesdale.

Strong Steed

Angus's spirit might be as bold as Merida's, but sometimes her exploits make him nervous, like when she follows the will o' the wisps. They're enough to spook any sensible horse!

LIKES:
- Adventures with Merida
- Galloping
- His warm stable

DISLIKES:
- Will o' the wisps
- Rings of Stones
- Anything he can't eat or that might eat him

Angus's shaggy coat keeps him warm in the harsh Scottish winters.

Best Friends

Merida received Angus when he was a foal and she was a little girl. Her friend and confidant, Angus is the best listener.

The Princess Manual

Teaching Merida to behave like a princess is easier said than done. Elinor knows exactly what her daughter needs to do. In fact, she could write a manual. But would Merida ever read it?

A Perfect Princess…

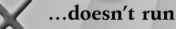

…doesn't gloat
or cross her arms and look pleased with herself—even when she beats her own father at archery or swordplay!

…doesn't dirty her gown
or tear the seams, rip the hem, or look as though she has just used her skirt to groom her horse.

…doesn't run
or jump, skip, climb, or race. She walks slowly and gracefully—which takes far too long in Merida's opinion.

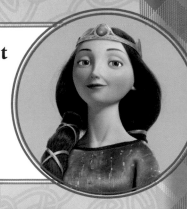

Mother Knows Best

Elinor isn't just being "bossy." She knows Merida will someday rule the kingdom and will need the lessons she is trying to impart. The problem is, Merida would always prefer to be doing something more adventurous.

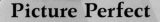

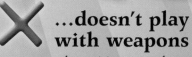

...doesn't play with weapons

...or beat visitors at archery, no matter how good she is. That would be showing off—something a princess never does!

Picture Perfect

Merida feels squeezed into a role she's not ready for. Something's going to break, and it's not just the seams of her gown!

A Perfect Day

Once in a while, Merida enjoys a day all to herself… with no lessons and no expectations. A day when she can just be herself, and anything can happen! How does she spend such a rare and perfect day?

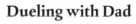

Dueling with Dad

After a hearty breakfast, Merida enjoys a spot of swordplay with her father. She's fast, agile, and sharp-witted!

Wandering in the Woods

Exploring the forest around the castle, Merida lets her imagination run away with her. Sometimes she spooks herself out.

Conquering a Crag

Legend says only the ancient kings were brave enough to drink from the Fire Falls, but Merida fearlessly climbs to the craggy top and quenches her thirst.

Speeding on her Steed

Galloping on Angus over the hills and through the glens, Merida feels as free as the wind.

Aiming to Win

The ping of her arrows is music to Merida, who can hit a target bullseye while galloping on Angus.

Sneaking a Snack

Warm muffins are the perfect snack after a day outside. It's nice to munch without lectures about table manners.

Perfectly Happy

Merida returns home windblown, exhilarated, and full of stories about her adventures. Tomorrow will bring more dull lessons, but for now she's perfectly content.

Clan Macintosh

Wiry, proud Lord Macintosh and his athletic son are fierce fighters. But young Macintosh tends to tear up when things don't go his way. He looks fearless, but he quickly resorts to slapping and sobbing during a battle. There's no crying in swordfights!

A sore loser, Young Macintosh has a childish temper tantrum, which doesn't win Merida's admiration.

Did You Know?
Ancient Scottish warriors painted themselves blue to appear intimidating.

Lording It
Lord Macintosh likes to boast. When he introduces his son at the ceremony, he tells the crowd that young Macintosh defended their land from Northern invaders and vanquished a thousand foes with his sword.

LIKES:
- Using his flail to crack walnuts—and heads

DISLIKES:
- Undershirts

"At least we have hair!"
Lord Macintosh

Father & Son
This dynamic father-son duo is quite an impressive team. They both favor big, heavy weapons and a wild-haired look. If victories were decided on fierce looks alone, they would always win.

LIKES:
- Showing off
- Winning

DISLIKES:
- Being ignored by Merida
- Losing

Macintoshes never wear undershirts. Their tempers keep them warm enough.

Lord Macintosh favors a flail for fights, but his son thinks his sword gives him a "sharper" image.

Show Off
Young Macintosh is used to crowds of adoring young ladies screaming every time he tosses his long flowing locks. His ego is as big as his sword.

Clan MacGuffin

Strong as a bull and always dignified, Lord MacGuffin is determined that his son will become Merida's husband. It's too bad the shy young man isn't quite as enthusiastic! He'd rather be tossing the caber—or even snapping it in half—than throwing kisses.

People from the other clans find the MacGuffins' strong accent very difficult to understand.

"But we haven't had dessert yet." Lord MacGuffin

Brawn not Brains

Lord MacGuffin claims that his brawny son once vanquished two thousand foes with his bare hands. The proud papa may be exaggerating a bit, but the burly boy certainly is strong enough to throw two dozen foes at once.

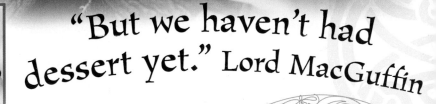

Royal Debt

Fergus once saved MacGuffin's life by stopping an arrow meant for him. MacGuffin returned the favor by aiding Fergus in his first battle with Mor'du.

Did You Know?

Young MacGuffin speaks in a dialect known as "Doric," which was commonly spoken in medieval Scotland.

Lord McGuffin has a very deep voice that booms around his castle. His laugh can almost be heard throughout the land!

Father & Son

Young MacGuffin looks up to his strong, stoic dad and eagerly follows his example when it comes to engaging in a hearty knock-down brawl or a hair-raising bear hunt.

Young MacGuffin has started trying to grow a beard like his father, but he is not quite there yet.

LIKES:
- Reliving past deeds of glory

DISLIKES:
- Hearing Fergus sing about Mor'du—again!

LIKES:
- Tossing cabers
- Swinging benches

DISLIKES:
- Archery
- Public speaking

Clan Dingwall

Surly and suspicious, Lord Dingwall can get prickly if anyone makes fun of his son. He prefers fisticuffs over conversation as a means of settling a disagreement. Like the other Lords' sons, Wee Dingwall is keen to please his father, but really isn't that eager to marry quite yet.

Games of strength and skill aren't what Wee Dingwall enjoys. He would rather play the bowstring like a harp than shoot arrows.

Wee Warrior

As Lord Dingwall boasts about his son, all eyes fall on a muscle-bound warrior standing nearby. Then the real Wee Dingwall steps into view!

Kiss My Kilt

Modesty isn't always the best policy. Hot-tempered Lord Dingwall is quick to let others know what he thinks of their opinions about his boy.

"Go on! Say it to mah face!" Lord Dingwall

Did You Know?
Lord Dingwall is the oldest of all the Lords. He is also the surliest of the uproarious bunch!

LIKES:
- Arguing

DISLIKES:
- Jests at his son's expense
- Underwear

Lord Dingwall has a hot temper and a ruddy complexion from the cold Highland climate.

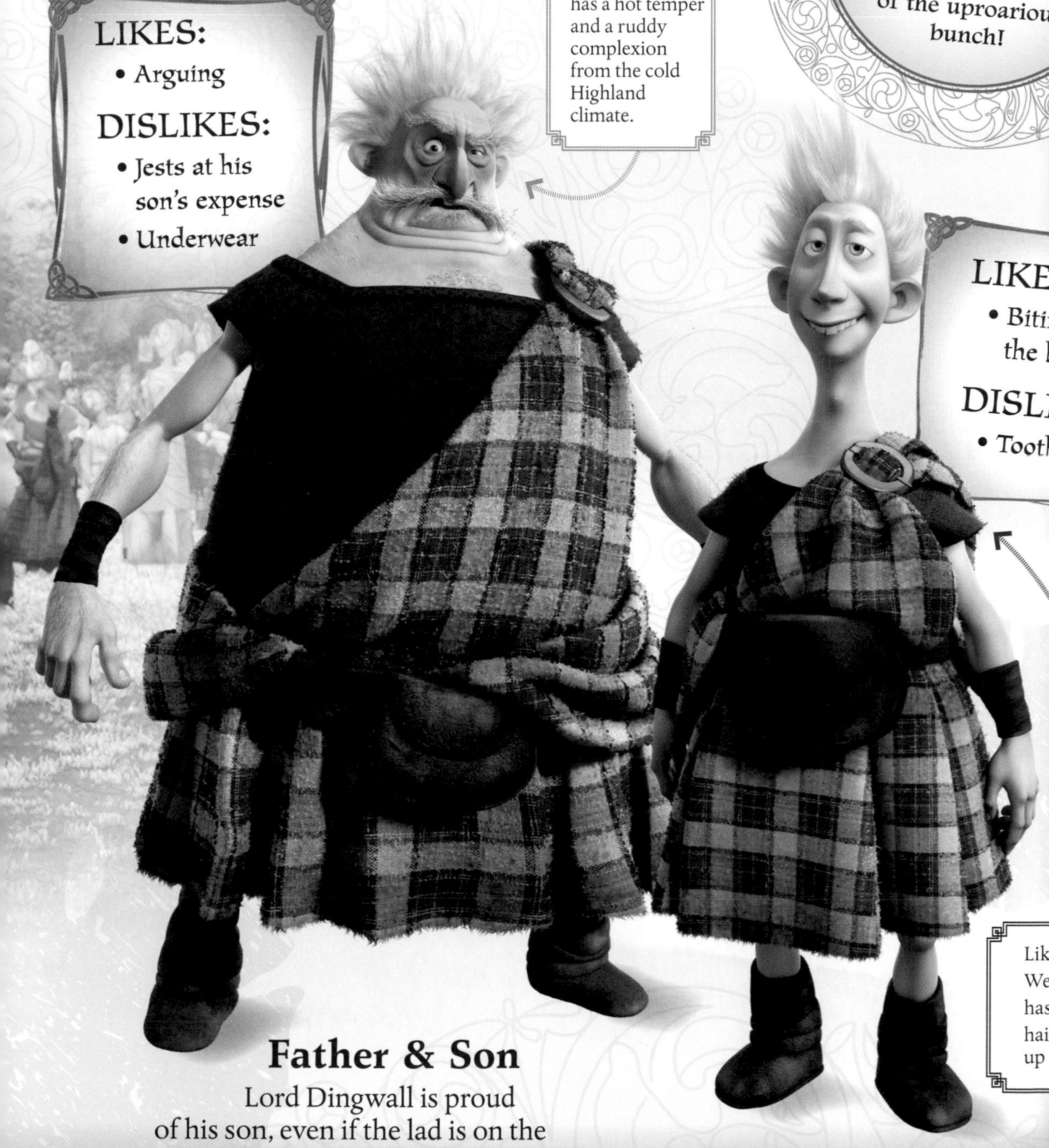

LIKES:
- Biting the bullet

DISLIKES:
- Toothaches

Like his father, Wee Dingwall has wild, wiry hair that stands up on end.

Father & Son

Lord Dingwall is proud of his son, even if the lad is on the scrawny side. Wiry, eager Wee Dingwall proves to be a frenzied fighter with a surprising battle style: he bites.

Who Suits Merida?

Fergus and Elinor think Merida is mature enough to choose a suitor and organize for some local lads to be presented to her. Each lad has something to offer Merida, but she doesn't agree. Merida doesn't dislike the suitors that are presented—she dislikes the idea of getting married right now! Let's hear what the lads have to say...

Parental Approval

Most parents worry that they won't like the suitor their daughter chooses. For Elinor and Fergus, the worry is that Merida doesn't even want one!

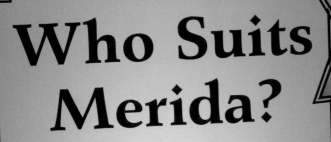

1 Macintosh

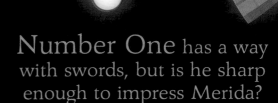

Number One has a way with swords, but is he sharp enough to impress Merida?

Q: How would you start a conversation on a first date?

A: Ask the girl to tell me everything she admires about me.

Q: What are you looking for in a girl?

A: She has to know how to shine a sword.

Q: If a girl doesn't pay attention to you, what do you do?

A: Cry. Jump up and down. That usually gets me noticed.

Merida pulls her wimple down over her eyes when Number One takes to the floor. She is not in the mood for this.

2 MacGuffin

3 Dingwall

Will it be suitor **Number Two**, the stocky lad with a talent for snapping logs?

Q: What's your idea of a *perfect* first date?

A: (in Doric) A caber-tossing competition. Lasses *love* watching me throw logs.

Q: How would you compliment your date?

A: (barely audible) Tell her she's large enough to hold up a bridge.

Q: What would you talk about on a first date?

A: (mumbled) Logs?

Feisty **Number Three** may be small, but he's determined to leave his mark on the kingdom.

Q: What qualities attract you in a girl?

A: Strong *teeth*.

Q: What do you think is your most attractive feature?

A: My hair. Lassies love my windblown look.

Q: Who would you ask for advice about dating?

A: My Dad. He's a real charmer with the lassies.

Merida peeks out when she hears Number Two snap a log. She she has to laugh at his attempts to impress.

Merida's relieved when Number Three turns out not to be a huge warrior, but she's shocked when Wee Dingwall bites a Lord!

Great Hall Brawl

The clan gathering goes awry when the Lords and their sons insult each other. The Great Hall erupts. Everyone seems to be enjoying the chance to punch each other. After all, if you can't clonk your friends, who can you clobber?

Fergus shouts unabashed encouragement at bashers and bashees alike: "Nut 'em! Nut 'em!"

It's only a matter of time before the King throws himself into the rumpus.

"Brawl! Bagpipes, kick in!"
Lord Dingwall

Calmly, Queen Elinor stops the chaos with an icy look that makes the burly brawlers feel like shamefaced schoolboys.

Let the Games Begin!

The sound of bagpipes mingles with shouts and cheers as the clans dance, eat, drink, and watch impressive feats of power. Merida usually enjoys the annual games, but this year it's different. Whichever suitor wins a contest of her choosing, will win her hand in marriage. And she will lose her freedom!

Since the 11th century, games have played a traditional part of clan gatherings in Scotland.

A Suitable Contest

Events like the caber toss and hammer throw require strength. But for the suitors' competition, Merida chooses a game of skill that she can win—archery!

COMPETITOR	PTS
 MERIDA	30
 DINGWALL	10
MACINTOSH	2
MACGUFFIN	0

Stunned Lords

Merida hits the target and then all the suitors' targets. The Lords can't believe it! Their sons have been outdone by a lass! It really gets their kilts in a twist.

Horrified Mother

It takes a moment for Elinor to realize what Merida is doing. "I forbid it!" she shouts as Merida draws her bow. But, but Merida has no intention of stopping.

Archery Enemies

When Merida defies tradition and wins the archery contest, Elinor is furious and shouts: "You don't know what you've done!" Merida has always trusted her mother, but right now, she doesn't care.

"I expect you to act like a princess!" Elinor exclaims as she throws Merida's prized bow into the fire. Merida sees this as a huge betrayal.

"Do you ever bother to ask me what I want?" Merida

Love & Conflict

Elinor and Merida were once the best of friends. But daughters grow up and gain their own minds. Conflict is natural, but for Merida and Elinor it could break their special bond forever. If only they could appreciate and understand their differences.

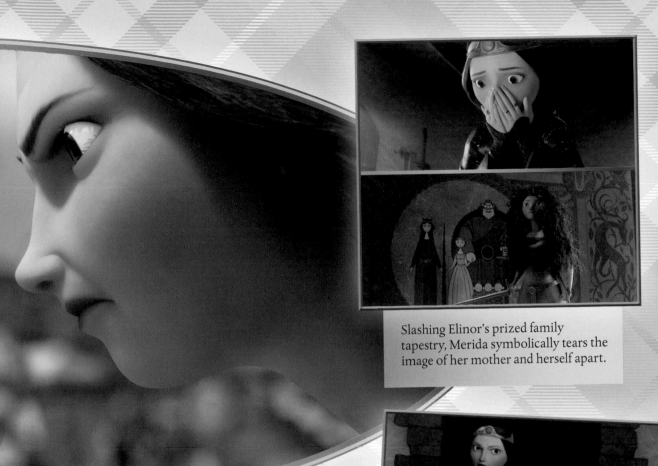

Slashing Elinor's prized family tapestry, Merida symbolically tears the image of her mother and herself apart.

Hurt by each other's angry words and actions, neither mother nor daughter can back down. They cannot see the situation through each other's eyes.

Special Bond

Merida remembers happy times when she and her Mum enjoyed tender moments together. They still love each other dearly, but something needs to change so they can bond and become close again.

Beckoned by Magic

Merida has heard the stories about the strange creatures who inhabit the Scottish Highlands. She thinks they're just myths—until she stumbles upon a stone circle and finds a group of will o' the wisps who seem to be waiting for her.

Ring of Stones

Upset and unhappy, Merida rides Angus into the dark hills and suddenly finds herself at a stone circle she has never seen before.

No one knows who erected the stone circles in Scotland, or why, but, like Merida, anyone who sees them is awed.

Mischievous Lights

Some say will o' the wisps like boggy areas. Others say they are attracted to ancient places like the stone circle where Merida first sees them.

"Why would the wisps lead me here?"
Merida

Flickering Guides
Although she has heard stories of will o' the wisps leading travelers astray, Merida follows them. But are they leading her to danger—or her destiny?

Stone circles like this one have stood in Scotland for thousands of years—long before Merida's time.

The wisps lead Merida and Angus to a craggy, spooky looking cottage. The wisps aren't welcome here, but could this be where Merida finds a solution to her situation?

The Witch

When Merida wishes for a spell that will change the way her mother sees the world, the Witch eventually agrees to make one. But Merida needs to learn to love her mother, flaws and all, or the spell will never be broken. Will she figure this out? The Witch's riddle is the only clue she has.

The Spell Cake

After much boiling, bubbling, toil and troubling, the Witch gives Merida a small cake. How can a cake change anything? Merida soon finds out!

"Fate be changed, look inside, mend the bond, torn by pride." The Witch

The Witch's cauldron bubbles and glows before creating a blinding flash.

Did You Know?

In Highland Scottish folklore, there is a specific spell to change a human into an animal. It is known as fith-fath and is supposedly a verse chanted aloud.

Crafty Carver

Posing as a whittler of wood, the Witch has filled her cottage with carvings of bears. Merida promises to buy every carving in exchange for a spell. That's a deal!

Unusual Facade

The old crone is reluctant to admit she is a witch. At first she insists she is a woodcarver who knows nothing about casting spells, even though her broom is sweeping—by itself!

The Witch's crow companion may look like taxidermy, but he is quite talkative!

LIKES:
- Carving wooden bears
- Cooking up spells and spell cakes
- Bargaining and bartering

DISLIKES:
- Being called a witch—she's a whittler of wood
- Visitors—unless they buy something
- Conjuring where she carves

The Witch wears a cape as green as the moss on a stone.

Becoming Bears

Merida wants a transformation to occur, but she wishes to change her mother's mind, not her shape. A change will eventually take place inside both of them. The process will prove more daunting than Merida can possibly imagine.

Peace Offering

When Merida offers her mother a piece of the spell cake as a "peace offering," Elinor is pleased and touched. She thinks the cake indicates a change in their relationship. Little does she know...

Feeling Different?

Merida watches her mother anxiously. Is the spell changing her? How does she feel about the marriage? But all Elinor feels is ill.

"B-B-EEEAAARRR!"
Merida

New Identity

At first, Elinor doesn't understand why Merida is screaming about a bear. Then she sees herself in the mirror, and understands the terror.

Mum-Bear tries to keep her crown on, but this doesn't last long!

Three Little Bears

Merida needs the triplets' help sneaking Mum-Bear out of the castle. In return, she lets them eat anything in the kitchen. Naturally, they see the remains of the spell cake...

The triplets don't seem fazed by their new look. Now the busy little bruins just have even more ways to make mischief.

Mum-Bear

Even as a bear, Elinor retains her queenly demeanor and sense of decorum. But the longer the spell lasts, the more Elinor is in danger of forgetting her human nature and remaining a bear forever.

CASTLE ESCAPE

The spell cake Merida gave her Mum turned her into a bear. Merida wanted her to change, but not like this! She must find the Witch and get the spell reversed. But first she and Mum-Bear need to escape the castle before her father sees her—or she'll end up stuffed.

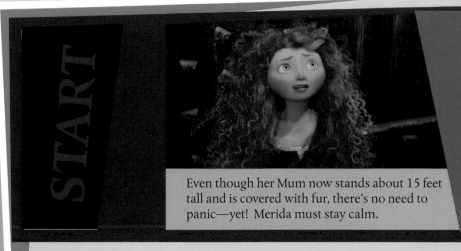

START

Even though her Mum now stands about 15 feet tall and is covered with fur, there's no need to panic—yet! Merida must stay calm.

Mum-Bear ducks into the trophy room as the clansmen rush past. The triplets see her, but they're not worried.

Merida must find her siblings to help lead her father and the others away from Mum-Bear.

They're through the door and out of the castle. Now, Merida and Mum-Bear can go find that pesky Witch and get the spell reversed.

Fergus sniffs "bear," and he's on the hunt. Merida has to get Mum-Bear down the hall without being seen.

The Lords think Fergus is only imagining a bear, but he's the King, so they'll follow him. Quick, Merida—go another way!

Maudie the kitchen maid sees Mum-Bear and screams. Fergus hears her!

In her confusion and panic, Mum-Bear comes to a dead end. Merida must go back and help her.

Mum-Bear and Merida should give each other a bear hug after that escape act!

FINISH

Dark Discoveries

As Merida and Mum-Bear search the wilds together, they discover some positive things about each other. But dark secrets also lie hidden in the lost regions of the forest. And danger lurks closer than they think.

Ruined Hopes

After hours of wandering, Merida and Mum-Bear stumble upon the abandoned wreckage of the Witch's cottage. The Witch is gone, and with her has gone their hopes of breaking the spell.

Once a confident queen with the answers to everything, now Mum-Bear has no idea what to do.

Fishing Buddies

As Merida and her mother fish, they enjoy each other's company for the first time in a long while. Mum-Bear gains respect for Merida's skills and spirit, and Merida glimpses her mother's playful side. They're very different, but they start to appreciate the differences.

Ancient Ruins

A will o' the wisp leads Merida and Mum-Bear to an ancient stone ruin. It lies half swallowed by the earth, a feeling of dark mystery surrounding it.

As Merida explores the ruins, she falls into a vast chamber littered with bones—it's Mor'du's lair.

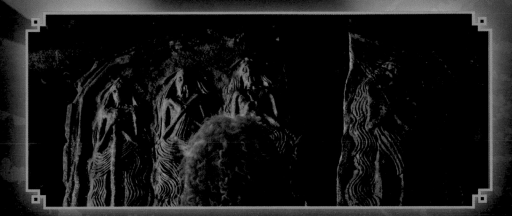

Lost Kingdom

In the shadows, Merida sees a stone carving of four princes. It is split in two—like the tapestry. She starts to piece it all together. Elinor's legend of the lost kingdom is true. And the spell has happened before!

Mor'du

There are creatures so fierce that hearing their name sends a cold chill through the blood. The legendary bear, Mor'du is one. Enormous and full of rage, he roams the wilderness, striking without warning just like a vengeful demon.

The Legend Lives

When Merida asks the Witch for a spell, the old crone recalls a prince who once asked her for the strength of ten men.

Merida is the first to realize that the prince in her mother's legend, and the prince for whom the Witch once made a spell are the same. And that he was changed forever into the demon bear, Mor'du.

Fearless Fergus

Fergus seems to be the only person who isn't terrified by Mor'du. He wants revenge for his lost leg. He is determined to face the bear again.

Mordu's fur is littered with the weapons of fallen enemies.

Terrifying Encounter

Standing in the ancient ruins, Merida hears a growl. Turning, she sees Mor'du. Though she shoots arrow after arrow at the monster bear, nothing can stop him.

Elusive Bear

No one knows how long Mor'du has stalked the kingdom. Sightings of the ferocious beast are very rare. When he does appear, it's as if from nowhere. Those who have seen him talk anxiously of his mighty roar and terrifying teeth.

As Merida scrambles for safety, Mum-Bear pulls her out, then tips a stone over the opening.

"Come taste my blade, ye manky bear!" Fergus

Did You Know?

Before the triplets were born, Fergus defended Elinor and Merida from an attack by Mor'du when they were on a family picnic.

Being Brave

Believing that she must mend the torn tapestry to break the spell, Merida sneaks back into the castle with Mum-Bear. The clansmen are fighting—as Elinor predicted. Merida must stop the battle before the kingdom is torn apart, too!

Speaking Up

Merida tells the Great Hall she is prepared to choose a suitor, but to her surprise, Mum-Bear shakes her head. As her Mum mimes what to say, Merida tells the Lords that the queen wants young people to find love in their own time.

Hidden in Plain View

As Merida enters the Great Hall, Mum-Bear poses as a stuffed bear. The angry Lords demand to see the queen at once. She's much closer than they realize!

As she listens to Merida speaking to the Lords, Mum-Bear feels proud of her daughter's courage.

Fergus vs. Mum-Bear

When Fergus sees Mum-Bear, he thrusts Merida aside and draws his sword. Mum-Bear's instinct is to protect her "cub." She charges, and Fergus wounds her. She runs from the castle.

Pleading with Dad

Desperately, Merida tries to convince her father that the bear is Elinor. But Fergus has no patience for nonsense about witches and spells—not when there's a bear on the loose.

Locked In

Believing the bear has killed Elinor, Fergus is bent on revenge. He won't risk losing Merida, too. Ignoring her pleas, he locks her up and gives Maudie the key.

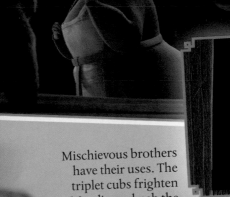

Mischievous brothers have their uses. The triplet cubs frighten Maudie, and nab the keys to get Merida out of lockdown!

Bear Hunt

Fergus and the clansmen chase Mum-Bear to the Ring of Stones, tether her with ropes and close in. But as Fergus lifts his sword, Merida's arrow deflects his blow. She is prepared to fight to save her mother.

Breaking the Spell

Once again, the Ring of Stones is the stage. Fergus has battled with Mor'du before but now it's Mum-Bear and Merida's turn to take on the beast. Merida must save her Mum and find a way to break the spell for good.

At the Ring of Stones where Merida's adventure began, bonds are restored and ancient spells are broken at last.

Repairing Tears

After yanking the heavy tapestry from the wall, Merida begins stitching its torn edges. She can only hope that the triplets will free her in time to save her mother.

Merida continues to sew even as she and the triplets ride Angus to the Ring of Stones.

Last Battle

Mor'du suddenly appears, wanting to fight all of them. Mum-Bear manages to break free and throw the beastly bear against one of the giant stones. Her love for Merida has given her the strength she needs.

"I just want you back. I want you back, Mummy." Merida

Love is All

When Merida drapes the mended tapestry over Mum-Bear, nothing happens. Weeping with disappointment, she tells her Mum that she loves her. Her words repair the rift between them, and the spell is broken.

True Bravery

The spell has been broken and the kingdom is at peace. Merida has not just won the right to wed when she's ready, she has also won her mother's understanding. In turn, she has learned what it takes to be truly brave.

Merida and her Mum have been working on a new tapestry together. It will always remind them of their special bond.

Now Merida is free to get back to her archery and sword fighting practice.

Suits Them

Three happy suitors set sail for home. Thanks to Merida's courage, they are all free to follow their hearts and someday wed whomever they please.

LONDON, NEW YORK, MELBOURNE,
MUNICH, AND DELHI

Project Editor Victoria Taylor
Editor Julia March
Senior Designer Lynne Moulding
Managing Art Editor Ron Stobbart
Publishing Manager Catherine Saunders
Art Director Lisa Lanzarini
Associate Publisher Simon Beecroft
Publishing Director Alex Allan
Production Editor Andy Hilliard
Production Controller Shabana Shakir

First published in the United States in 2012 by
DK Publishing
375 Hudson Street, New York 10014

12 13 14 15 10 9 8 7 6 5 4 3 2 1
001-184024-May/12

Published in Great Britain by Dorling Kindersley Limited.
A catalog record for this book is available from the Library
of Congress.

ISBN: 978-0-7566-9232-2

Color reproduction by Altaimage
Printed and bound in USA by Lake Book Manufacturing, Inc.

The publisher would like to thank the following:
Satvir Sihota, Clive Savage, Toby Truphet, and Mark Richardson
for additional design assistance; LeighAnna MacFadden, Kelly
Bonbright, Steve Purcell, Leeann Alameda, Cherie Hammond,
Clay Welch, Desiree Mourad, Holly Lloyd, Silvia Palara, Jesse
Weglein, Angie Mistretta, Magen Farrar, Dawn Rivers, Tasha
Harris, Tim Zohr, Brian Tanaka, and Britney Best at Pixar
Animation Studios; Victoria Saxon, Maria Elena Naggi, Heather
Knowles, Scott Tilley, Scott Piehl, Winnie Ho, Shiho Tilley,
Chelsea Alon, and Lauren Kressel at Disney Publishing.

Discover more at
www.dk.com